DROWNING IN DAYDREAMS

by Emerson Van Wie

NEW GAME+

Shapeless as water
Free as a bird
High tides, do not falter
These wings you birthed
Explore the universe
This realm yours to traverse
Fall in love with something new
As I once did, with you

LYING TO MYSELF

Once, we were in love
It wasn’t real, but that wasn’t the point
But I lied so hard I somehow believed it
At least for a little while
You told me my voice was nice
I still think about that sometimes
And when we danced
You looked into my eyes
I wonder what you saw
Did you love me too?

HAUNTED HOUSE

I live amongst these faded walls
Tied to the memories
My house is full, but all of them are out to get me
But how is a house so full so silent and empty?
I keep grasping at time
Hoping to free those that haunt me
I see them in the window
Dancing ephemerally
I want to leave my house and toss away my key

DREAMERS

Collectively beautiful
This one's for you, dreamers
You all shine so bright
And though we may not see each other
I know you're out there
Shining your brightest
My light may escape me
But I know you believe in me, too
The memories we've conjured
Take me back
To the imaginary darkness
To crafting the world in our image
We could've been something great
The universe tore us apart
It said we should shine separate from one another
For together, we would've been too bright
Please sustain your shine
For your sake, and mine.

STASIS

A song

Sending me to the past

I see the moon as it sinks

Yet, still, I stay

Time surrounding me

That sacred stardust

Accept my stasis

Progress me through your eyes

3000 years could pass

Success still escaping my grasp

What would I think of me now?

COUNTING ON YOU

Potions flow along these cavern walls
Increasing my stats as time goes on
My mind on my mission
A party there to support me
A lonely vagabond among unlikely heroes
Optimism flows even in the darkest of times
The taro cards on our side
A large bear sleeps near the exit
Relax.
Step aside.
We all make it through, in the end.

ATLANTIS

My beloved treasure
Hours, countless
Sour my lips with yours
Doors opened and closed
Dance with me along the riverside
Find your Galdin Quay
Days go by, even years
Yes, finally I can fly
I'm coming your way
With wings too frail to cross the sea

MAGICIAN'S DESIGN

My beloved treasure

Hours, countless

Sour my lips with yours

Doors opened and closed

Dance with me along the riverside

Find your Galdin Quay

Days go by, even years

Yes, finally I can fly

I’m coming your way

With wings too frail to cross the sea

MAGICIAN'S DESIGN

Help me create true magic
We share so much but know so little
Conjure me a new creation
Show me what your eyes wish to see
Why is talking so easy?
Is it our similar taste in women?
Or just our rhythm in sync to a metronome?
Whatever it is, I'll fight with you
Through this war we call life

YIN AND YANG

You were everything and nothing
Who I wanted to be
And who I hated
And when you were always there
It felt like a toxic gas
Slowly choking me from the inside
Why were things so difficult?
I can’t feel how I did back then
And for that, I’m happy at least

PAIR

The two of us
Fire and Ice
You shine so bright
Melting my mask
Burn bright, my flame
I'll just freeze here
Crying alone
My tears crystal
My mind feels just
Intoxicated
It's not your fault
No, little flame
It's just the ghosts
and ghosts to be

THIRD TIME'S THE CHARM

Roadside confessions
Keep me in silence
Maybe let some time go by
I should've learned my lesson
We're so casual now
Never text me first
I didn't deserve it
But when you did
My heart would flutter
This wall I can't climb
Each sentence rushed
Every hand I crushed
I like dark chocolate with my coffee
Just something to remember me by

JESTER'S SEVENS

Broken butterflies
Please spill me your secrets
Descend to me
All of your deepest feelings
I'd comment on every post
Play footsies with the cosmos
Chisel my stone
I'd be any image
Anything to be heard

OOPS

Your strange state of being
The puzzle of your cognition
Like looking through a kaleidoscope
Somehow navigated through the maze
And found a way out
Your gravity held some close
Was my gravity just as strong?
Could you let me know?

WATER TEMPLE

This cracked mirror before me
Everyone tells me to throw you away
As hard as I try, I could never
I still see myself in you
No matter how many times I've grown
The man in the mirror
So young, but still broken
I wanted to be you once
But I've grown since then

SOUTH

Gentle humming of the radio
Playing every song we never made
Crystalized honey staring back at me
The red string of fate truly attached
Speaking every truth
Your pink aura intoxicating my mind
Let’s leave this crowd
Isolate ourselves
Feel this ray of light between us
Well, maybe another time

EDEN

Please take me to Eden
If not all, then only just a piece
Wherever that may be
Live on without me
I'll just stay here
Slowly sinking
This is my Rapture
Years of pain on this canvas
Sinking to the depthss

JANUARY

“Fuck you” written in blood
A broken strawberry, too
That’s where we started
Wandering aimlessly
The most beautiful sight I’d ever seen
Until I saw you
I fell in love in Chinatown
I swam in your eyes
You helped me fly
Everything just a simulation
A slow dripping poison
I’m still grounded
No wings in sight

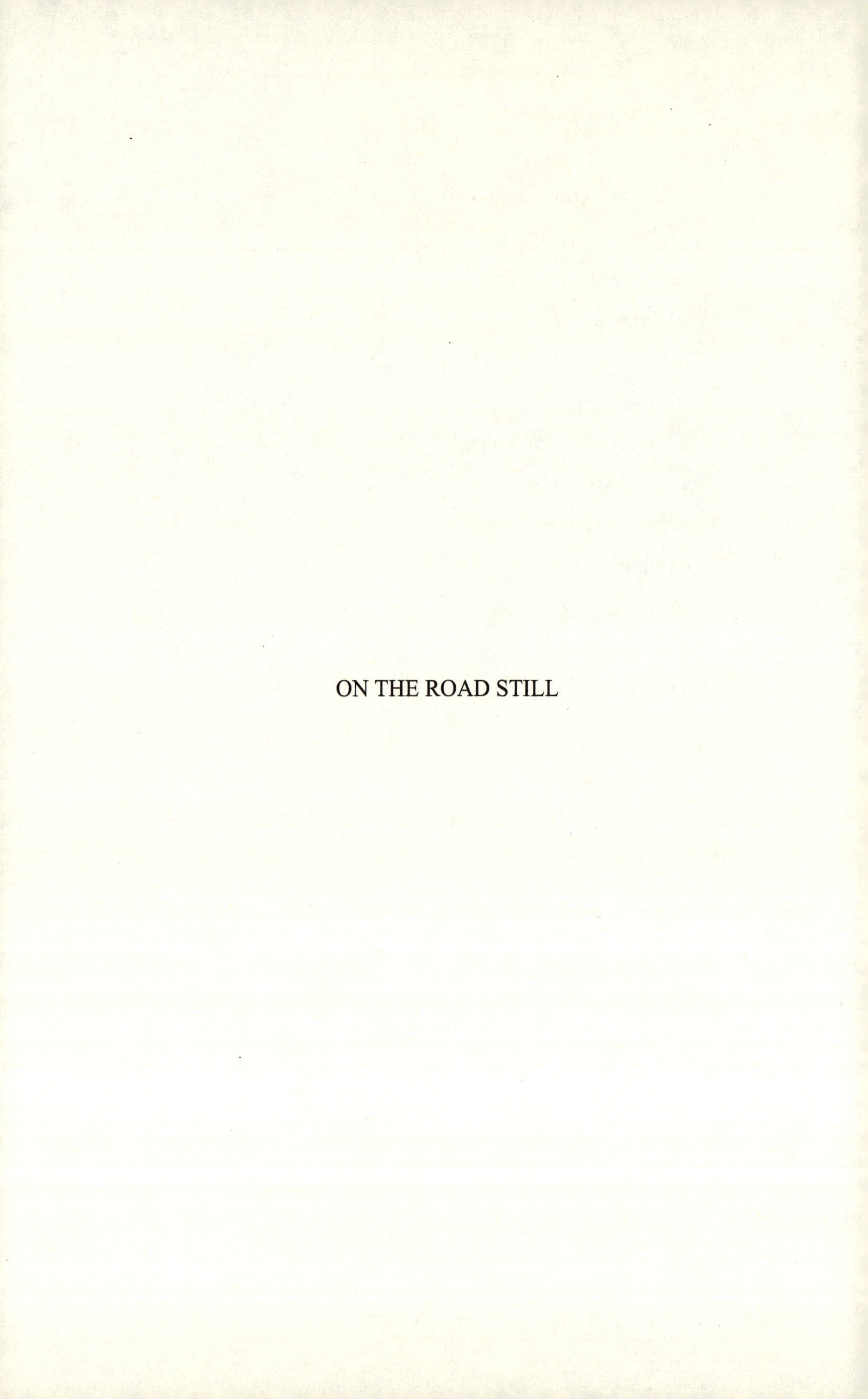

ON THE ROAD STILL

Learning to breathe

From these ashes you've been born from

Feeling the breeze

A warrior by his lonesome

What does he see? We never really knew

Until we're by the fire again

Tales from kingdoms every now and then

"But where was my story?"

He asked, a smile in his inventory

I had no answer, nothing for him

I told him surely there was something

But no answer

He smiled again, ashes on his clothes

"You're my brother forever

even if we're not close."

BEYOND

Together we've traversed time and space
Floating above the ground
Inside of these pink clouds
You've shown me real magic
Made time stand still
Thank you, I really needed that

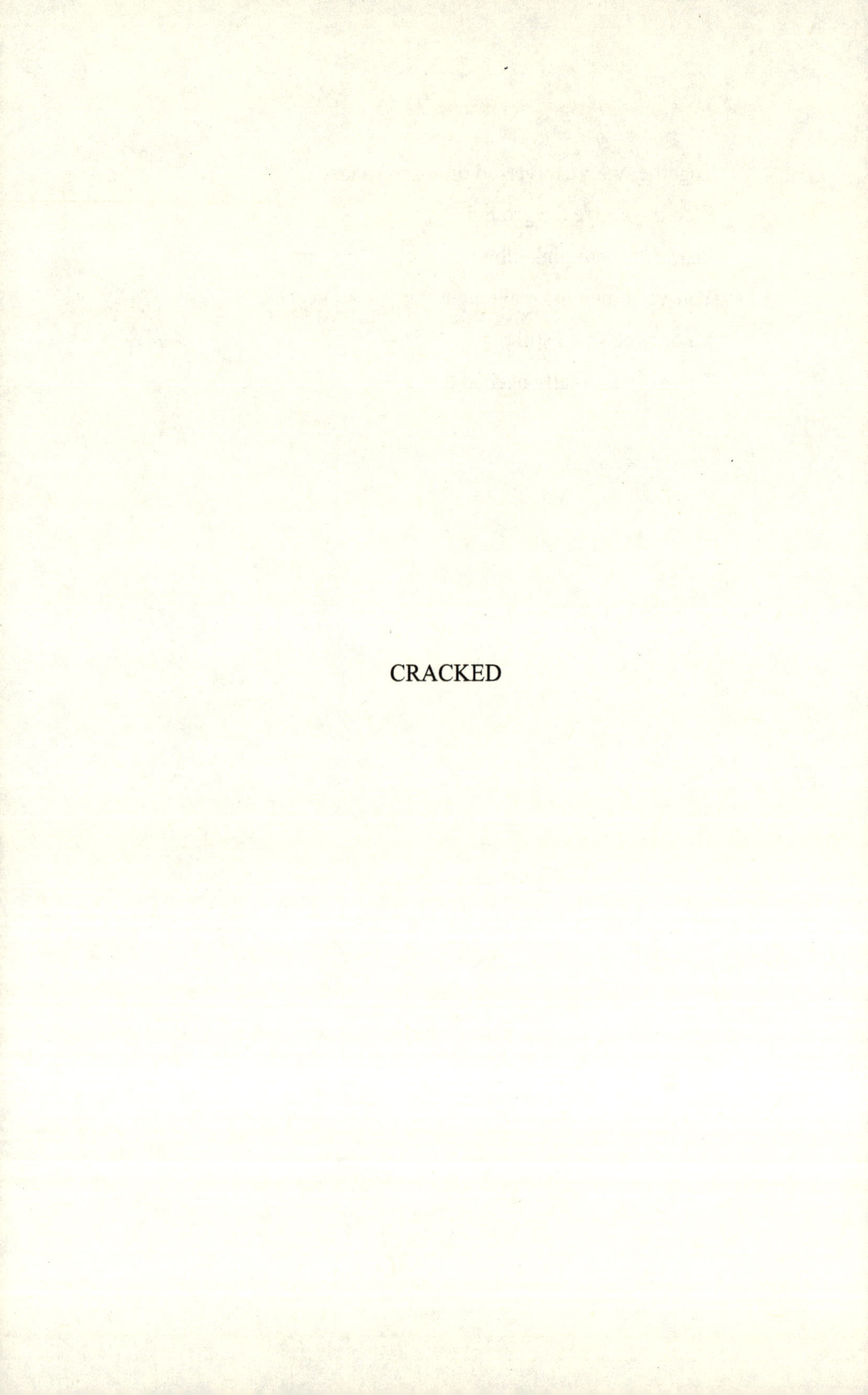

CRACKED

Honey stained eyes

The soul overwhelming

Golden hour as time seems to fly

Your presence trembling

Don’t be afraid of me

We’ve known each other for so long

Yet this distance, such a longing feeling

In parallel, we sing what was unsung

LOTUS

I stay inside my house
My windows open, but door shut
I water my garden thinking of you
Thousands of lotus petals
None quite as beautiful
Maybe one day you could see it too

FOIL

We meet again
Gravity that ties us down
Let me fly
I've traveled across the Earth
Yet here you are again
Always sinking us down
Shouldn't happiness be enough?
Why must you have everything
I'm alone again
Are you happy now?
You got what you wanted, didn't you?
This noose necktie you've shacked me with
I know it's not your fault
You want to be happy too
But I've found somewhere new
Finally, somewhere I belong
But we always meet again.

KINDRED

Eyes like depths of the sea
My kindred spirit
Just a tricky kitsune
Was everything an illusion?
Time passed us by I could feel it
But how is that possible
The kiss felt so real
But you vanished in an instant
Leaving me with false memories

DON'T OVERDO IT

As the years have gone by
One thing has never changed
As the moon rose each night
You kept a smile on my face
And as we sat across from one another
I always wondered what it would be like
To run away and live a fantasy
When your hands held mine
Or ran through my hair
I've never felt more myself
So I'll say it, I'd say it 1000 times

I love you more than life itself

RETRO

Living in the past

Almost like a photograph

Too bad, the future came too late

This isn't how it ends, though

I'll ride or die for you

Either reaper or by kaiju

Coffee stains paint my reflections

The words we use, our only weapons

Make me the best that I could be

Paint me in your retro sea

PAIN REINCARNATE

You see them as I do
But twisted, and deformed
A mirror in a fun house
I respect the average
But as they are
As you may see them
It never sat well with me
I would never be them
Or anything else you loved
For that matter
Why were you here so long?
When I was never welcome

SOS

(shine out of shield)

"What if the stars could reach for us?"

Do we really deserve that much?
A simple soul for some stardust
Stars are beautiful, I'm sure not
But you're much more stunning
Than stars wish they could ever be

GET IN LINE

I was first in line
Drowned out under the night sky
Just a caterpillar looking for some food
Above me, so many fireflies too
One day, I'd be like them, maybe
And then there was you, baby
Forcing me into my cocoon so young
Shows never seen, songs unsung
I was never special, under your hard drugs
I didn't know the sky was so full of lovebugs

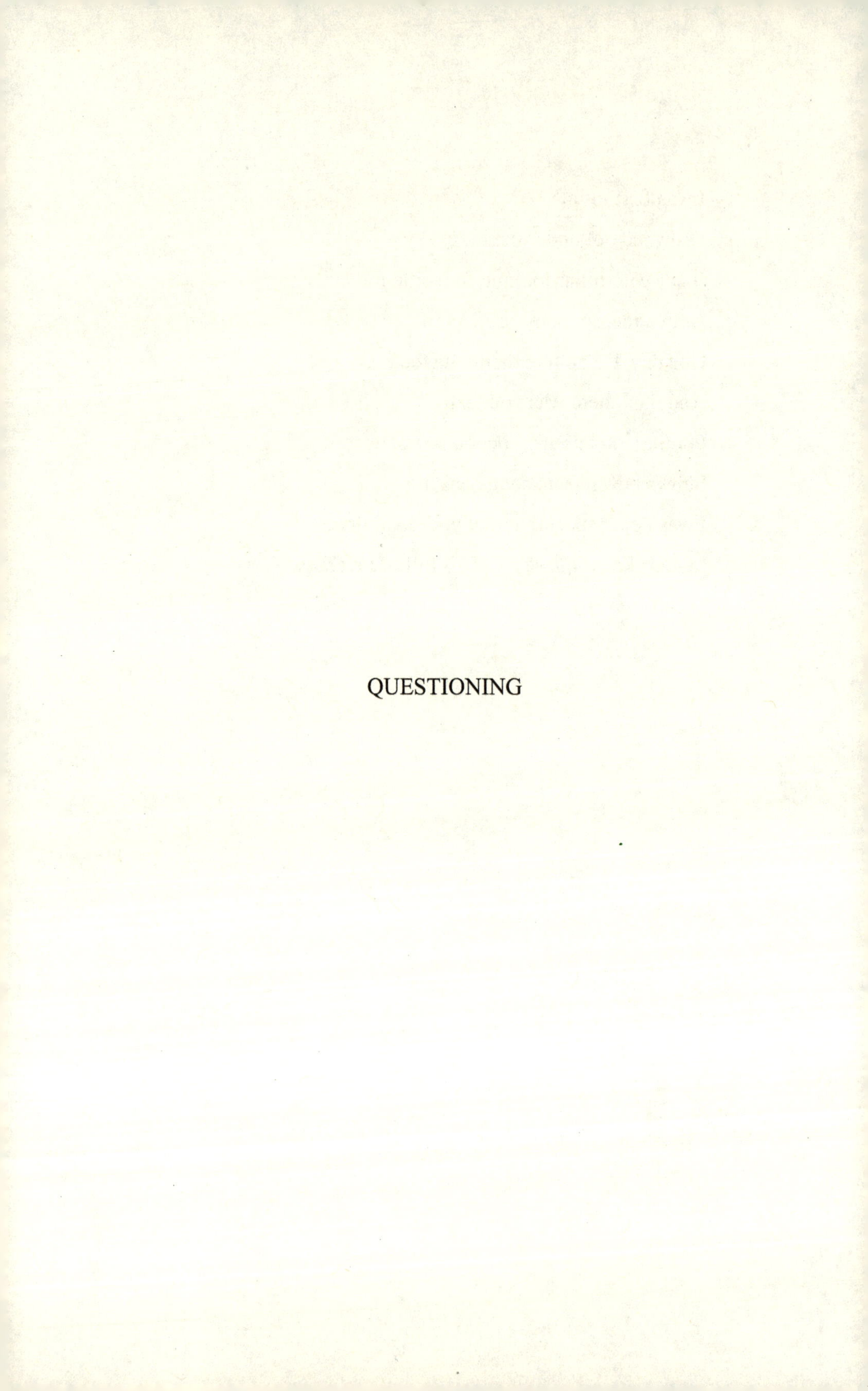

QUESTIONING

Why is there always a destination?

Why can't we just stay here?

Is there something wrong with finding comfort?

What are we trying to prove?

To who?

VALOR

Neon lights shine across a colossal sky
"What weapon was used to slay the witch?"
Tall tales told in bazaars that night
Sneak away silently, smooth as a satin stitch
Boats float bounded by their mechanics
An easy night ride now, no envy for me, though
Floated across and found Atlantis
Drift past, but never forget what we've seen
Time and space left traces of memories
Valor in the afterglow, a view that could kill
Follow the life, review it all, in time we'll see

LAGOON

This time in our aquatic mine
Bestow me my name
Finally an identity
A true name to go by
Something clever
But formless as clay
Sit with me
Beneath this tree that grants us purpose
That’s all a graveyard theory
I won’t let this get to me

LOST WOODS

Traverse this wasteland
Two bandits, side by side
Steal from those less fortunate
Sit upon our throne of blood diamonds
Listen to our story
Let’s drink until we forget
Forget these confusing times
Fly above what made us weak
“At last, the journey has come to an end”
And then, our story truly began

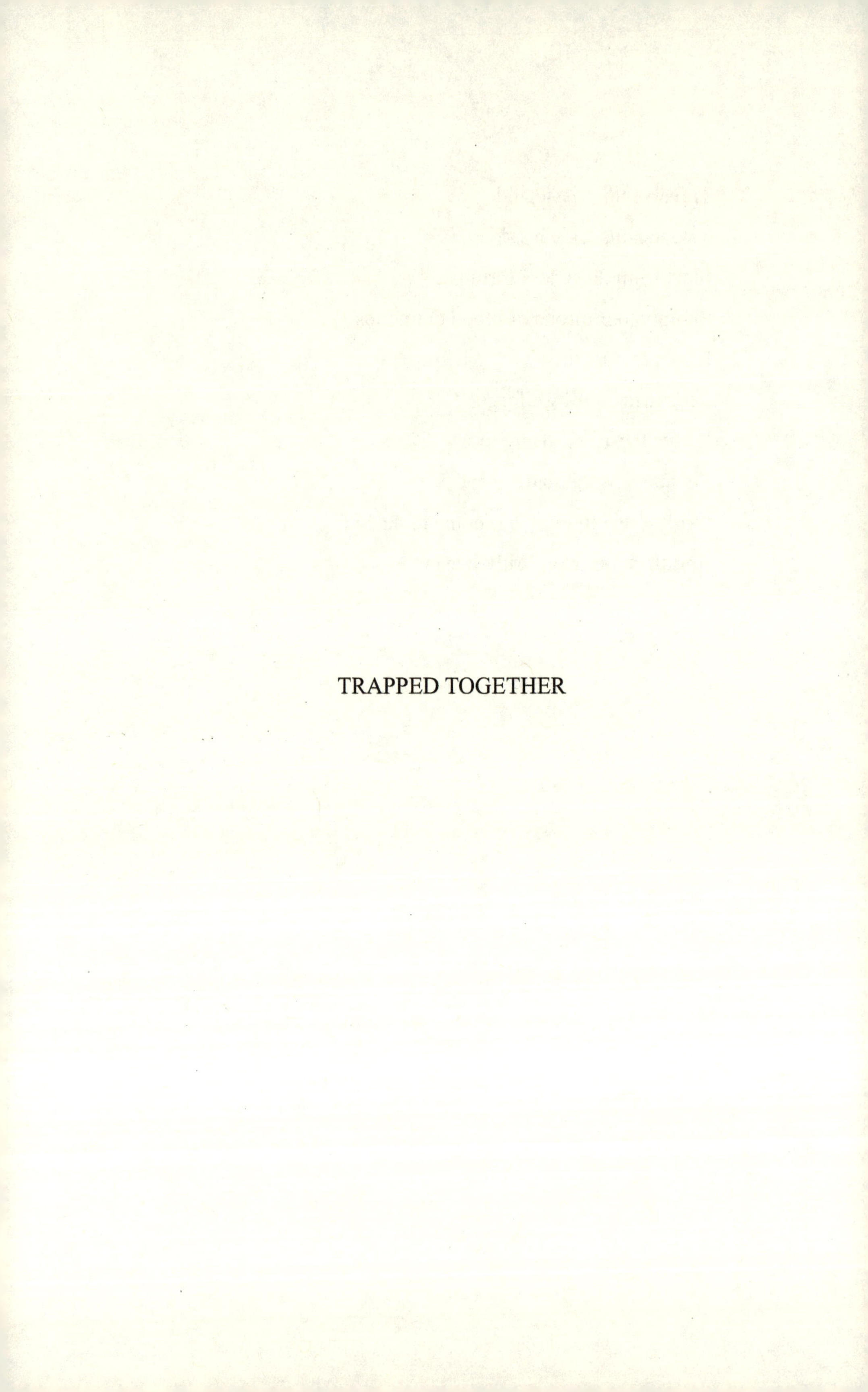

TRAPPED TOGETHER

The cold nights created me
I would bide my time in those walls
We were just numbers to them
We didn’t care though, did we?
You broke me from my shell
Blacking out from the attention

3 GNOMES

The three gnomes tried to distract me
Deadly and dark, but so exciting
Existing only as entertainment, I comply
Completely concrete in their approach
Actually, I appreciate their rhythm
Relaxing and really lively
Laughing, I learn to forget
Forget feelings too hard to handle

MORE THAN I COULD ASK FOR

Roulette of life
really plays some crazy games
What are the odds we were born?
We exist at the same time
Across time and space
And yet no one even comes this close
Our twin flame
Over infinite parallel universes
Each one, we definitely meet
Even the divine couldn't have kept us apart

ONLY WHO?

White doves in the horizon
How did we get here?
A faint confusion of self
A moment of weakness
I'm in too deep
We share something
A piece of me
Something I can't seem to shake
I could never say no
An aftershock of loneliness
Maybe I'm still too weak

See you tomorrow, I guess.

MONA LISA

She was art

A painting worth 1000 words

Each one sweeter than the last

But a painting is only 2D

Blame me, for not exploring further

Into your third dimension

I was trying to breathe when I was underwater

Even though I wasn't aware

I hope it didn't hurt too bad

I know you cried for me

I'm really sorry.

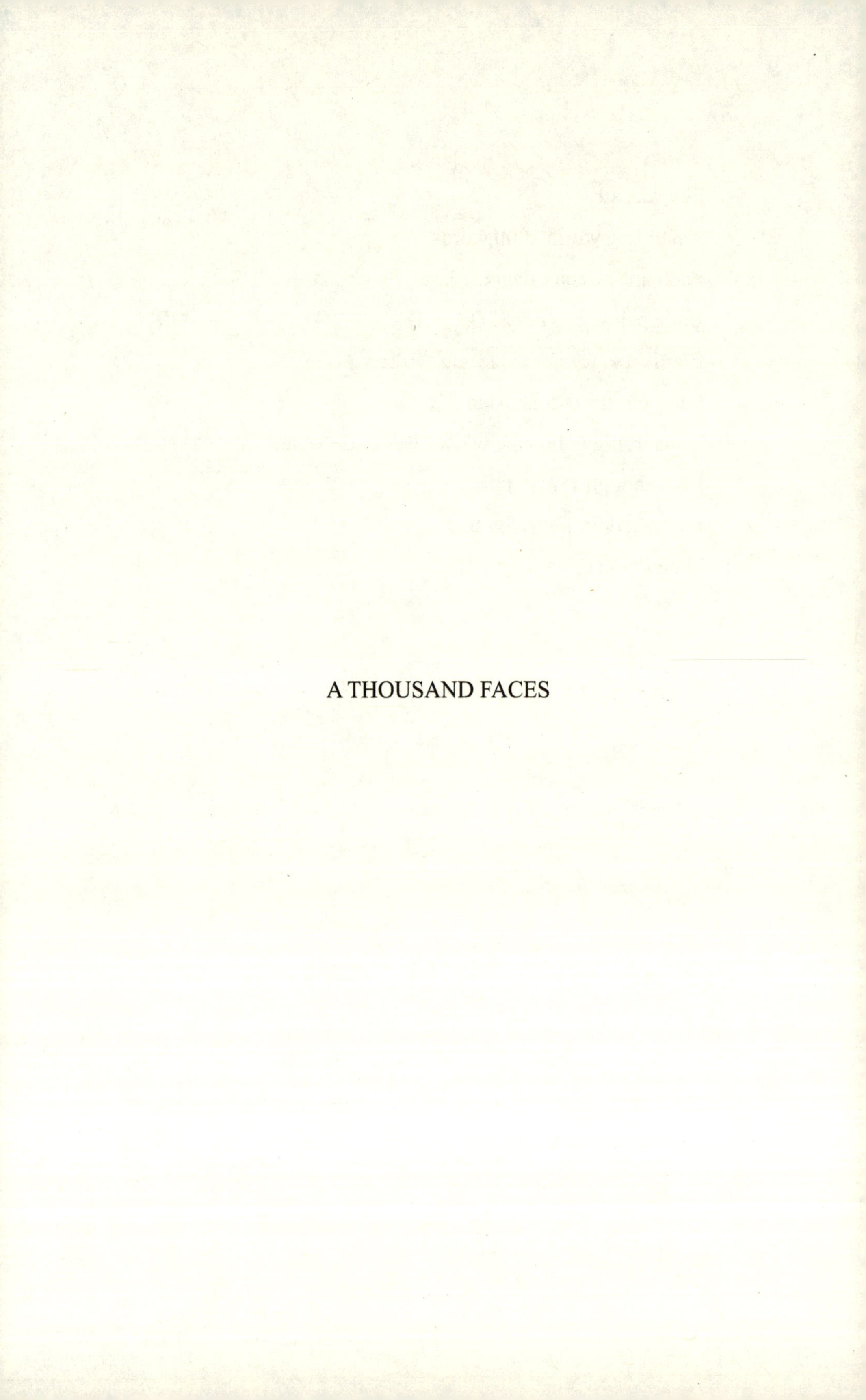

A THOUSAND FACES

Fall back

A universe we've found ourselves

An infinite void feeling occupied

Read my heart, you're tongue tied

Tell me what you find

I keep drifting feeling misaligned

Thoughts straining those who stay inside

When will I find one to stay by my side

It could be loose, but I'd hold on tight

My love dancing by the riverside

TRULY

Nostalgia fogs my memories
From N64 nights
To summers everlasting
These feelings so true
Even down to this identity
A true name
A love letter to a younger self
Staying true
To playground trials
I hope he finds himself again
One day.

BENEATH THE MASK

You dawn that veil, so mysterious
Put me in your world, create a new me
Two worlds never bound to cross
How can we shift our gravity?
Desire brings me closer
You drown me out with walls of great fire
Why do you hate me so?
A sky, fluttered with crows
It was never about being first
It was about being yours.

FAIRY LIGHT

Why shine so bright?
Oh, beacon of light
What drives you to succeed?
Your wisdom, shared with me
Shelter me in the rain
Survive the nights of snow
Please, beacon, guide me through this pain
Until next time, sustain your shine though

OR SOMETHING ORANGE

I lay here

Staring into the infinity between us

This unhealthy obsession

Thoughts of 1000 impossible meetings

I don't know the real you

I know your sapphire eyes and pastel hair

How can that be all?

This love between us

Cuts infinity in half

My eyes never met

My soul never explored

Maybe it's better that way

SNOW IN DECEMBER

A voice soft as cotton
Eyes pierce like ice
Shouting *"Dog!"* in the streets
I miss the way you speak
Your words, nothing but nice
Are you keeping your eyes on me?
The writing's on the wall
My hand always within reach
Just give me a call.

POTENTIAL

Why can't we speak before midnight?
Am I not worth your daylight?
I only earn the scraps of your cognition
The last fleeting little life
Please, fill in with your puzzle pieces
Your shape never meshing
Because your place was with me
These spots so specific
As unique as your soul
See? They'd fit just right
If you just made it through the night

PHASE 2

Will we be forever?
Yes she said
A feeling I thought I could treasure
“Will we be friends instead?”
How did I upset her?
Spent a few years in my head
Shed more tears than feathers
Then came you, just to pretend
Using me at your leisure
“Will we be friends instead?”
It happened again.

MY PRIDE

The kindness you've shared
Gentle Lioness
Where would I be without you
How would I feel
Maybe stuck in stasis
Or lost in space
I should thank you
For mapping my darkness
Paving my way to the sky
And being there when I finally fly

You

Yes, this has all been about You
Ironically, You probably didn't read this far
You're really impatient
And always too bored to commit
I've always hated that about You
But there was always more
A flame beneath your wings
Powers I always wished were mine
I hope You're happy now
I hope You remember me
Even if it's just as another book on the shelf
I'll still love You
Whoever you are.

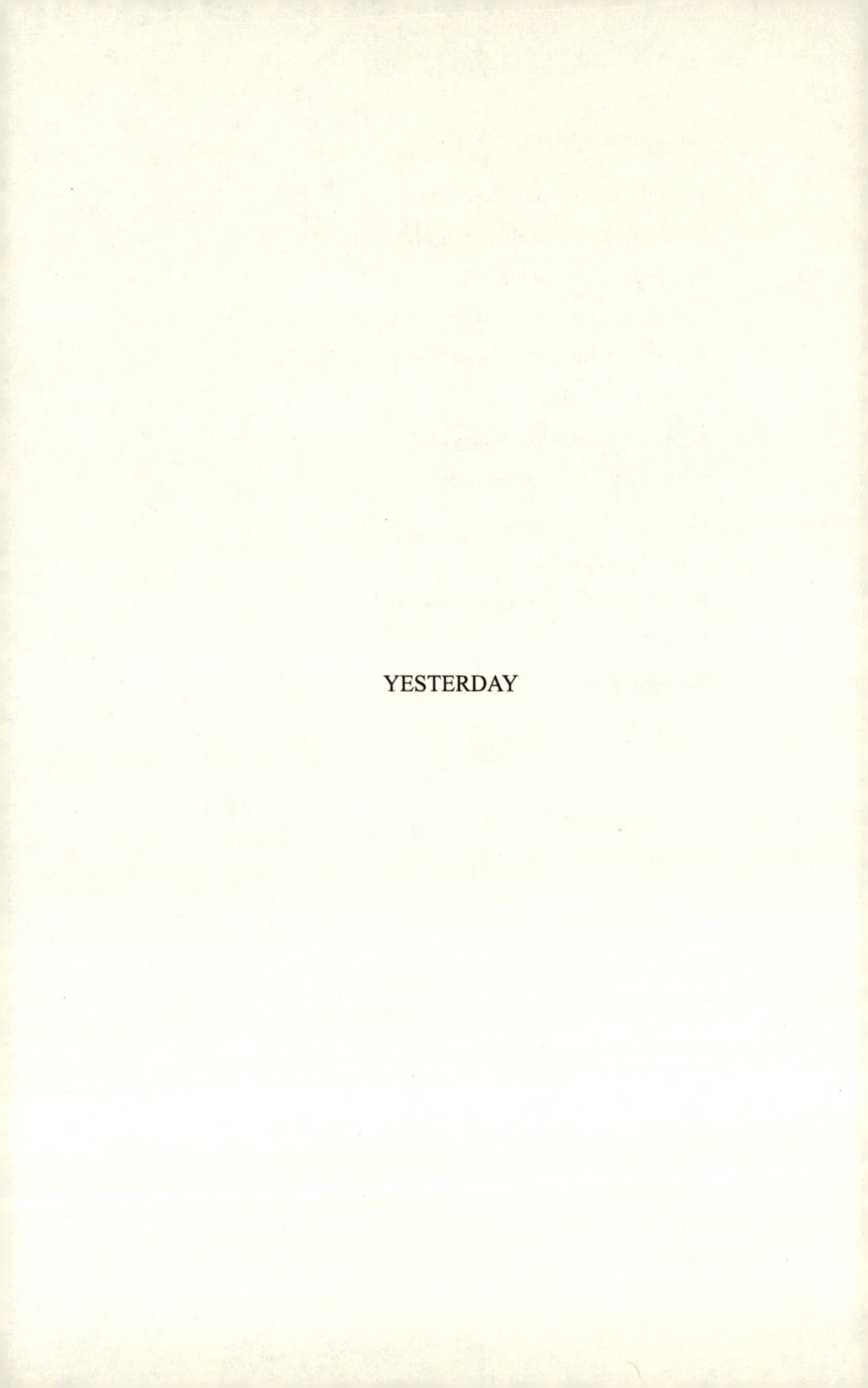

YESTERDAY

Why don’t I feel the aftershocks?
Every earthquake before was so clear
Destruction from high magnitude
So what’s happening now?
Do I have no more ground left?
Or have I just not landed yet?
My house is still in one piece
Only the glass shattered
But nothing that can’t be fixed

ROUGE

If I could steal your problems away

I would do it in a heartbeat

But alas, I'm useless again

BOXCUTTER

Perfectly flawed
My soul escaping
A walking shell
Trying to feel
Intrusive thoughts
Hollowed out
This candy aisle
The walls caving in
Can’t breathe
No room for me

MAJORA

Oh what I'd give
just to see the past as it was for
just 5 seconds, I would
cement them into eternity.
Every kiss that I had rushed, every
goodbye not knowing that
they were my last, even
if nothing could change, I would
sacrifice my life just to see
you again

LILACS AND GREENS

The infinity between us
Lasting only inches
Our souls bruised purple
Memories of the greenest trees
Oh the life we could have lived
Delicate daydreams
Sweet as honey but fragile as glass
Another golden sunset, both here and there
Nothing comes close to the bond we share.

QUEEN OF HEART

An heir to a throne
A successor of wealth and knowledge
The one to reap rewards of those before
Red flags plucked from the ground
Replaced with scars
Please slay the dragon to the east
I cannot accompany you
For I am too frail
Success on this quest
Towers of wealth and joy
Please bring peace to this kingdom

VOIDWOKEN

I thought I was the thief
So how is it that you stole *my* heart?
Not in like a romantic way
But in a very literal sense
I guess not too literal
I'm still alive after all
It is quite sad though

The best part about you now
Is forgetting you existed.

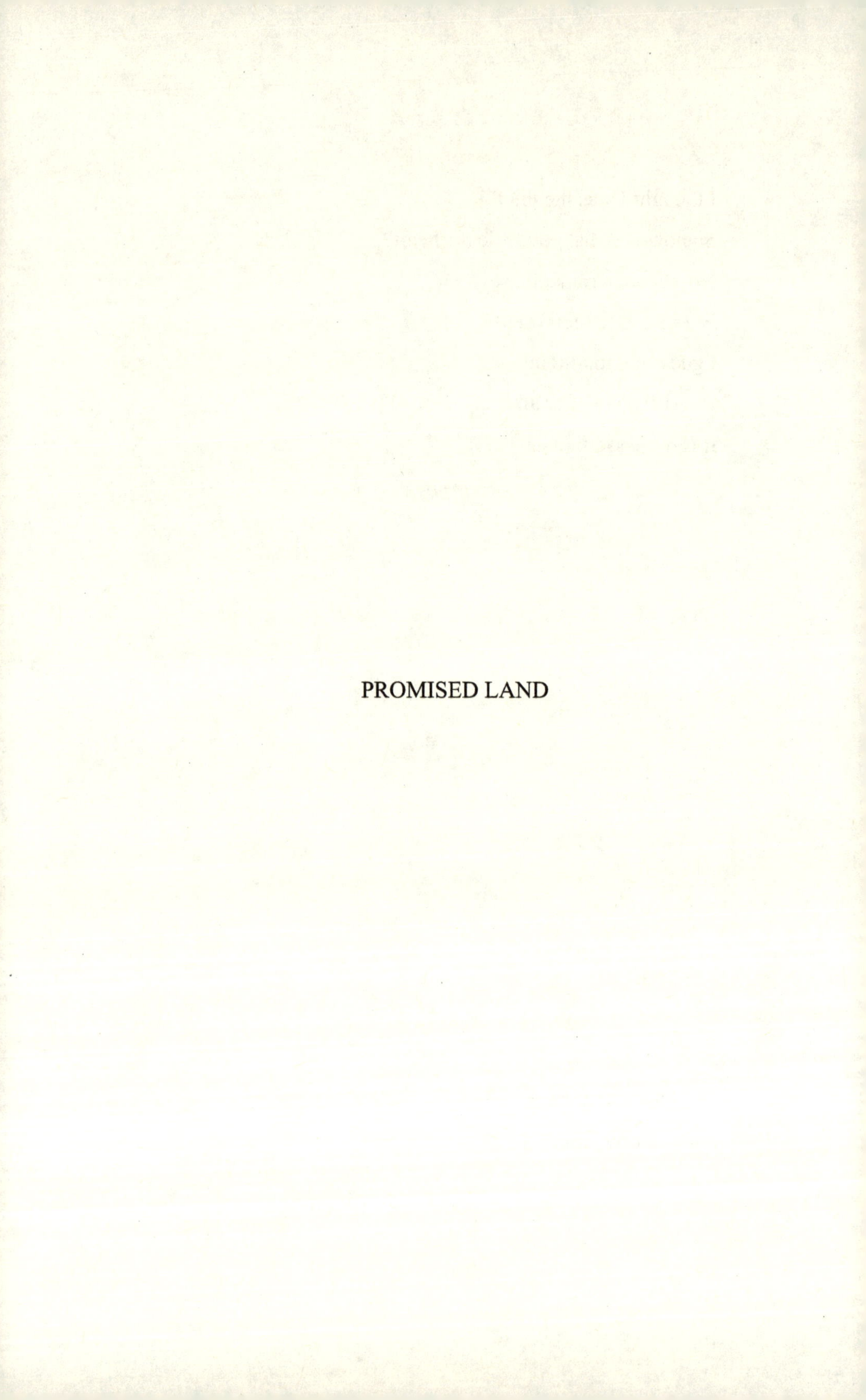

PROMISED LAND

Forget what you've seen here

Everything was a ruse!

All an elaborate lie

I promise I'm doing fine.

This tome is nothing but stories untold

Sitting in the wellspring of life

Wounds heal, souls replenish

There's so much I wish I could tell you

Just so you'd know that I can thrive

Keep the best me in your memories

Because I know, even now

I'm much better than he is.

www.ingramcontent.com/pod-product-compliance
Lightning Source LLC
LaVergne TN
LVHW041118150826
845673LV00007B/2101